# NOAH'S ARK

## Illustrated by Tony Morris

Brimax · Newmarket · England

**O**nce, long ago, there lived an old man called Noah. He was a good man who loved God. One day, Noah started cutting trees into planks of wood. Many people stood and watched him, in order to see what he was making.

Noah had not told anyone why he was cutting the wood. Even his wife and his sons did not know. At last, after several days, they realized he was making a very large and strong boat.

"How will it float when there is no water nearby?"
"Why are you making it?"
"What is it for?"
These were the questions Noah's family asked him. Noah said, "This is my ark. It will have a door in the side and a roof. It will have a window and three decks."

"God has told me to make the ark," said Noah to his wife. "He is going to send rain to cover the land. His people have been wicked and so every living thing will die. We must go inside the ark with our sons and their children. We must take two of every kind of animal with us. When the water comes, the ark will float and we will all be safe."

"We will need food for ourselves and food for the animals," said Noah's wife. So Noah, his wife and their three sons began to make plans for their stay on the ark. Sacks of grain and salt were stored on the ark. Barrels were filled with fresh water for drinking. Hay and straw were laid in the ark for the animals.

They found two of every animal and loaded them into the ark. There were elephants, lions and camels. There were dogs, cats, birds, snakes and even mice and insects.

Noah could see the rain coming so he closed the doors. Soon, huge, black clouds filled the sky and the rain began to fall. Day after day it rained, until the land was covered by water. As the water rose the ark began to float. The rain fell for forty days and forty nights.

At last the rain stopped and there was a strong wind. But the land was covered with water for five months. There was very little room for the animals. Noah and his family waited patiently for the water to go down.

Gradually the water
went down. The ark
came to rest on a
mountain called Ararat.
Noah looked out over
the water. He wondered
whether it was safe to
leave the ark or not.

Noah decided to send
out a raven. It did not
return. "I will wait a
little longer," said Noah.

A week later Noah sent out a dove. But the little dove flew back to the ark for some food. He waited another week then he sent the dove out again. As night fell Noah saw the dove returning to the ark. In its beak it held a green olive leaf. Still Noah waited. The next week the dove did not return. "It is now time to leave the ark," said Noah.

The door of the ark was opened and Noah and his family came out. The animals and birds were glad to be free again. God had saved Noah and his family from the flood. They all gave thanks to God.

Across the sky was a beautiful rainbow. This was a sign from God that he would never flood the whole world again.

All these appear in
the pages of the story.
Can you find them?

dog

Noah

elephant

Noah's wife